Forgiveness

The Choice That Sets You Free

DEBBIE BARR

AspirePress

Forgiveness: The Choice That Sets You Free

Copyright © 2024 Deborah Barr
Published by Aspire Press
An imprint of Tyndale House Ministries
Carol Stream, Illinois
www.hendricksonrose.com

ISBN: 978-1-4964-8356-0

The views and opinions expressed in this book are those of the author(s) and do not necessarily express the views of Tyndale House Ministries or Aspire Press, nor is this book intended to be a substitute for mental health treatment or professional counseling. The information in this resource is intended as a guideline for healthy living. Please consult qualified medical, legal, pastoral, and psychological professionals regarding individual concerns. Tyndale House Ministries and Aspire Press are in no way liable for any content, change of content, or activity for the works listed. Citation of a work does not mean endorsement of all its contents or of other works by the same author.

All Scripture quotations, unless otherwise indicated, are taken from the Holy Bible, New International Version,® NIV.® Copyright ©1973, 1978, 1984, 2011 by Biblica, Inc.® Used by permission of Zondervan. All rights reserved worldwide. www.zondervan.com. The "NIV" and "New International Version" are trademarks registered in the United States Patent and Trademark Office by Biblica, Inc.®

Scripture quotations marked NLT are taken from the Holy Bible, New Living Translation, copyright ©1996, 2004, 2015 by Tyndale House Foundation. Used by permission of Tyndale House Publishers, Carol Stream, Illinois 60188. All rights reserved.

Scripture quotations marked ICB are taken from the International Children's Bible®. Copyright © 1986, 1988, 1999 by Thomas Nelson. Used by permission. All rights reserved.

Scripture quotations marked ERV are taken from the Holy Bible: Easy-to-Read Version (ERV), International Edition © 2013, 2016 by Bible League International and used by permission.

Author photo by Melinda Lamm. Cover photo: Pop Tika/Shutterstock.com. Other images used under license from Shutterstock.com.

Printed in the United States of America
010923VP

Contents

Introduction

Forgiveness: The Big Questions

FORGIVING OTHERS IS SOMETIMES EASY— *you stepped on my toe. No big deal.* But if you have been deliberately insulted, betrayed, or violated in some painful, life-altering way, forgiveness can be very, very difficult. The more outrageous the offense, the harder it can be to forgive, and the more questions it may raise:

- How can you forgive an offense you cannot stop thinking about?

- Should you forgive someone who doesn't ask for your forgiveness?

- What if the person doesn't even care that you were hurt by what they did?

- Does forgiveness mean you have to trust the person again, as if the offense never happened?

This book will help answer those questions by giving you a glimpse into the reasons *why* God wants you to forgive. Many people do not realize that releasing others through forgiveness can actually benefit the forgiver in amazing ways. Even more amazing is the mysterious fact that God can bring something good out of even your most painful wounds.

On the pages ahead, you may just discover that there is more to forgiveness than you thought!

Chapter 1
The Truth about Forgiveness

"Forgive him? You've got to be kidding! There's no way."

"I'll never forgive them for what they did. It's unforgivable."

It's not hard to recognize the pain and outrage behind these words. Perhaps you've even said these very words yourself. If so, whatever hurt you deeply was likely unfair, undeserved, and incredibly unkind—or maybe worse, an act of greed or hatred, or even evil. And whether the offense was unintended or deliberate, minor or catastrophic, a wrong was done to you, the wound is painful, and you may feel entirely justified in refusing to forgive.

If that's how you feel, you are hardly alone. Many people who have been deeply hurt by the insults, violence, or betrayal of others have vowed, "I'll never forgive." If your pain has led you to that same decision, it's possible that you may believe that forgiveness means something it really doesn't mean.

Forgiving someone does *not* mean:

- that what was done to you is okay;

- that the person is not accountable for what they did;

- that your relationship with the one who hurt you must be restored; or

- that your pain doesn't matter and that you should "just get over it."

Before we take a deeper look at each of these false notions about forgiveness, it's important to first clarify what forgiveness really means.

The Meaning of Forgiveness

The most important fact about forgiveness is right there in the subtitle of this book: *The Choice That Sets You Free*. Those words are there for a reason! The truth is, the choice to forgive is not about, or for, the person who hurt you. Forgiveness is for *you*. When you choose to forgive, *you are the person who is set free*. Forgiveness releases you, the offended person, from the toxic effects of simmering resentment, bitterness, and thoughts of revenge. It only takes one person—the offended person—to forgive. This one-sided forgiveness, known as *unilateral forgiveness*, does not involve the person who caused the offense.

> The choice to forgive is not about, or for, the person who hurt you. Forgiveness is for you.

Unilateral forgiveness is not a feeling; it's a choice. Forgiveness is a decision to no longer hold someone's offense against them. It's the choice to cancel the debt it feels like they owe you. Many people find that forgiveness is easier to understand, and easier to do, when they think of it as releasing the offending person to God. The action of releasing someone may be easier to visualize than the concept of forgiveness. Either way, the result is the same. As author William P. Young so memorably phrased it, "Forgiveness is ... about letting go of another person's throat."[1] When we do that willingly and from the heart, we realize the truth of theologian Lewis Smedes's words: "To forgive is to set a prisoner free and discover that the prisoner was you."[2]

The internal freedom that results from forgiveness has been described in many ways. Pastor T. D. Jakes says that forgiveness is "a gift you give yourself." He explains, "Forgiveness liberates the victim." He says that forgiveness has less to do with what somebody else did and more to do "with your decision to move on with your life and not be continually victimized by rehearsing that issue or incident over and over again."[3] Pastor Tony Evans has similarly said, "Forgiveness keeps you from being hostage to something that the other person may never ever get right."[4]

> Unilateral forgiveness is not a feeling; it's a choice.

The word *jettison* also sheds light on the meaning of forgiveness. Jettison means to discard or get rid of something. In centuries past, when ships encountered a life-threatening storm at sea, the crew often had to jettison its cargo to lighten the ship. Throwing the ship's heavy cargo into the ocean gave those on board a better chance of surviving a violent storm. According to the Cambridge Dictionary, *jettison* also means "to decide not to use an idea or plan." In other words, you discard your original plan, presumably because you now have a better one. Forgiving is a decision to jettison the heavy cargo of resentment and bitterness from your life instead of continuing to live under the burden of their weight. It's throwing overboard the self-sabotaging plan to "never forgive" and replacing it with the far better, self-nurturing plan of forgiveness.

What Forgiveness Is Not

In light of what forgiveness really is, now consider some aspects of what forgiveness is *not*.

Forgiveness is not an eraser.

Erasers make things disappear. Forgiveness doesn't erase what happened or the imprint it may have left on your life. Forgiving someone is not saying that the consequences for what they did are now erased or that what they did was okay. It is not saying they are no longer responsible for what they said or did, or that they should not be held accountable. If a crime has occurred, forgiving what happened should never keep you from reporting it. A strong sense of justice can trap a person in unforgiveness if they think forgiveness is an eraser. Don't let that happen to you. Forgiveness isn't about excusing the person who hurt you; it's about giving you the peace of mind you deserve.

Forgiveness is not a blindfold.

A blindfold prevents you from seeing. While it is always right for you to forgive, do not confuse forgiveness with trust. Forgiving someone does not require you to now trust a person who has lied to you or about you, betrayed you, stolen from you, or harmed you. Stay unblinded to the truth of what happened, why it happened, and what it means for your life and your future. It's not wise to assume that because you forgave, "things will be different now." While forgiveness represents the change in *your* heart, nothing at all may have changed yet in that other person. John the Baptist once challenged the religious leaders of his day to "show by the way you live that you have changed" (Matthew 3:8 ERV). You can take the same "prove it" approach. Don't be too quick to trust again. Instead, wait and watch.

Forgiveness is not anesthesia.

Anesthesia keeps you from feeling pain. Forgiving someone is not denying that your pain is real or saying that it doesn't matter. It doesn't mean that you should suppress your pain or numb yourself to it, even if someone else pressures you to "get over it." (Pastor T. D. Jakes has said, "It's always easy to say 'get over it' when you're not the victim."[5])

While pain is never pleasant, it often has a purpose. Emotional pain alerts us to the fact that something is going wrong in a relationship. While it's smart to pay attention when the pain alarm goes off, it's never smart to let pain control your decisions. Forgiveness is a choice, a decision of the will. Don't let your pain keep you trapped in unforgiveness.

Forgiveness is not glue.

Glue binds things together. Forgiveness doesn't always put relationships back together—nor should it. In a best-case scenario, both people work together to resolve their conflict, forgive each other, and continue on with their relationship. Sometimes going through this process makes a relationship even stronger than it was before. This two-way conversation about forgiveness, known as *transactional forgiveness,* can reconcile a broken relationship. Reconciliation should always be the goal whenever possible. However, when there has been verbal or physical abuse, infidelity, or other serious harm, it may not be possible or safe to continue the relationship unless significant changes occur. Change takes time, and sometimes requires professional help as well. Forgive, yes, but protect your heart. Don't fling the door to your life wide open right away. Move back toward the relationship only after you have observed the changes that are necessary to repair the breach and restore the relationship. In situations where reconciliation cannot occur, forgiveness will free you to move beyond a toxic relationship.

> "It only takes one to offer forgiveness.... It takes two to reconcile."
>
> DR. HENRY CLOUD

Some of the false beliefs about forgiveness are due to the confusion that arises when trying to discern when to trust and how to reconcile with those we forgive. One of my favorite authors, psychologist Dr. Henry Cloud, makes three very helpful, clarifying points:

1. **"Forgiveness has to do with the past.** Forgiveness is not holding something someone has done against her. It is letting it go. It only takes one to offer forgiveness....

2. **Reconciliation has to do with the present.** It occurs when the other person apologizes and accepts forgiveness. It takes two to reconcile.

3. **Trust has to do with the future.** It deals with both what you will risk happening again and what you will open yourself up to. A person must show through his actions that he is trustworthy before you trust him again."[6]

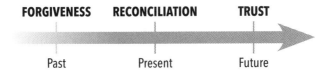

| **FORGIVENESS** | **RECONCILIATION** | **TRUST** |
| Past | Present | Future |

What Happens When We Forgive— and When We Don't

There is now plenty of evidence that forgiveness has a positive impact on both mind and body. More than fifty research studies have shown that forgiveness improves mental health. Studies link forgiveness to reductions in depression, anxiety, and major psychiatric disorders.[7] One study reported that "greater forgiveness is associated with less stress and, in turn, better mental health." The authors also noted that numerous other studies link forgiveness with "more happiness, better mental and physical health ... and less depression."[8] Research from Johns Hopkins indicates that forgiveness lowers heart attack risk, improves sleep, lowers blood pressure and cholesterol levels, and helps reduce pain.[9]

Unforgiveness has the opposite effect on physical and mental health. Holding onto grudges, nursing bitterness, and harboring resentments amount to keeping unforgiveness on life support. Constantly rehearsing the wrongs done to you keeps your wounds raw, painful, and unable to heal. In time, the toxic residue of unforgiveness seeps into every area of life, diminishing well-being in many ways. A Mayo Clinic article affirms this, noting that an unforgiving person might:

- bring anger and bitterness into new relationships and experiences;

- become so wrapped up in the wrong that they can't enjoy the present;

- become depressed, irritable, or anxious;

- feel at odds with their spiritual beliefs; and

- lose valuable and enriching connections with others.[10]

With this list in mind, consider this metaphor: Have you ever forgotten to take out the kitchen trash before you left on a long vacation? If so, as soon as you got back home and set foot in the kitchen, you were quickly greeted with a smelly reminder of the one chore you left undone. And then, for some inexplicable reason, what if you decided, right then and there, to *never* take out the trash? It's not hard to imagine the results of that decision. After a while, as the bags of trash piled up, the bacteria in the trash would multiply to the point that not only the kitchen but the whole house would be filled with the overpowering funk of decaying trash. And sooner or later, even the neighbors would notice! If you have ever been around a bitter, unforgiving person, you know why clinging to festering resentments is like refusing to empty the trash. When a person has become hard-hearted about forgiving, the toxic "aroma" of the resentments they harbor eventually permeates the atmosphere of all their relationships with others.

Forgiving hearts wear a different perfume! Just as emptying the trash makes a kitchen smell better, a heart emptied of its unforgiveness takes on a new, sweet-smelling fragrance. This lovely scent seeps outward to others, and unlike the noxious fumes of unforgiveness, it blesses those who breathe it in.

While forgiveness is not an exclusively Christian practice, forgiveness is the very heart of the Christian message. Second Corinthians 2:15 tells us that when Christ followers choose to forgive, they mirror the forgiveness of Christ, and God is well pleased with the lovely scent of that. The Living Bible paraphrases the verse like this:

> As far as God is concerned there is a sweet,
> wholesome fragrance in our lives.
> It is the fragrance of Christ within us,
> an aroma to both the saved
> and the unsaved all around us.

Forgiveness Matters to God

As I've mentioned, forgiveness is a choice. Anyone can choose to forgive. Age, gender, culture, or where a person lives makes no difference—forgiving others is a personal choice that is open to all, and beneficial to all who choose it. People can be motivated to forgive for many different reasons, such as mental or physical health benefits, to maintain family harmony, because of their moral or faith-based convictions, or simply because it's just what they want to do. Forgiveness is central to the Christian faith. So the most compelling reason why forgiveness should matter to Christ followers is that forgiveness matters to God. But just how *much* does forgiveness matter to God?

There are two great answers to this question. The first answer begins with the reasonable assumption that forgiveness must matter deeply to God because forgiveness was his idea! Forgiveness is "the gospel." Do you wonder what that means? I love how John Piper explains it so simply:

> What is the gospel? I'll put it in a sentence. The gospel is the news that Jesus Christ, the Righteous One, died for our sins and rose again, eternally triumphant over all his enemies, so that there is now no condemnation for those who believe, but only everlasting joy. That's the gospel.[11]

What is the "died for our sins" part? It's what God asked his only Son to do so that our forgiveness would be made possible. *That's* how much forgiveness matters to God.

The Unforgiving Servant

The second answer to the "how *much* does forgiveness matter to God" question is found at the end of this story that Jesus told:

> So God's kingdom is like a king who decided to collect the money his servants owed him. The king began to collect his money. One servant owed him several thousand pounds of silver. He was not able to pay the money to his master, the king. So the master ordered that he and

everything he owned be sold, even his wife and children. The money would be used to pay the king what the servant owed. But the servant fell on his knees and begged, "Be patient with me. I will pay you everything I owe." The master felt sorry for him. So he told the servant he did not have to pay. He let him go free. Later, that same servant found another servant who owed him a hundred silver coins. He grabbed him around the neck and said, "Pay me the money you owe me!" The other servant fell on his knees and begged him, "Be patient with me. I will pay you everything I owe." But the first servant refused to be patient. He told the judge that the other servant owed him money, and that servant was put in jail until he could pay everything he owed.

All the other servants saw what happened. They felt very sorry for the man. So they went and told their master everything that happened.

Then the master called his servant in and said, "You evil servant. You begged me to forgive your debt, and I said you did not have to pay anything! So you should have given that other man who serves with you the same mercy I gave you." The master was very angry, so he put the servant in jail to be punished. And he had to stay in jail until he could pay everything he owed.

This king did the same as my heavenly Father will do to you. You must forgive your brother or sister with all your heart, or my heavenly Father will not forgive you. (Matthew 18:23–35 ERV)

The "several thousand pounds of silver" that the first servant owed his master is translated as "10,000 talents" in other Bible versions. A talent was a measurement of weight and one talent typically weighed between 58 and 80 pounds. The 10,000 talents of silver owed to the master would have weighed about 375 tons! Each talent was equal to 6,000 days wages—about 20 years' pay for a laborer. The servant owed his master the modern equivalent of millions of dollars or, by one estimate, about 60 million days of work.

This servant had gone into the meeting with his master owing more than he could ever have repaid in his entire lifetime—and he came out of the meeting debt free! All was forgiven by his compassionate master. But instead of rejoicing and feeling overwhelmed with gratitude for the mercy he had been shown, as soon as he left the meeting he went looking for a fellow servant who owed him only "a hundred silver coins" (100 denarii, equal to 100 days' wages). Instead of taking the opportunity to "pay it forward" by showing the same mercy he had been shown, the forgiven servant grabbed his debtor by the throat and demanded immediate payment.

The lesson for us is that when we are unwilling to forgive as we have been forgiven, we are just like that ungrateful servant. We have forgotten that our sin had so indebted us to God that only the blood of his Son could repay what we owed. Whatever we are owed by our fellow humans, no matter how painful or offensive, is by comparison like a few pennies. Yet when our hearts are hard and unforgiving, it is as if we take that other person by the throat and demand payment.

(I'm guessing that William P. Young may have had this story in mind when he wrote that "forgiveness is about letting go of another person's throat.")

So how much does forgiveness matter to God? The answer is clear from the last sentence of the story:

> You must forgive your brother or sister
> with all your heart, or my heavenly
> Father will not forgive you.

Just as the king was willing to forgive the servant who owed him so much, God stands willing to forgive us— but only if we forgive our fellows! Does this mean if we fail to forgive others that God will revoke our salvation? No, of course not! Just as no child that is physically born into the world can ever be physically "unborn," once we are spiritually born into the family of God, we cannot be spiritually "unborn" either. This verse is not about our eternal salvation, but about the Lordship of Jesus in our lives while we are here on earth. That is, it's about whether we will do what he is asking us to do: forgive the one who has hurt us— even though it may be hard to do.

Some people are able to forgive very quickly. Others are so devastated by an offense that, for a while, their emotional pain keeps them from forgiving. Still others allow their emotional pain to harden their hearts and become their justification for refusing to forgive. Only God knows the depth of each person's pain and where they are in their journey toward forgiveness. Lewis Smedes said,

> There are instant forgivers, I suppose, but not many. We should not count on power to forgive bad hurts very quickly.... God takes his time with a lot of things. Why should we not take ours with a hard miracle like forgiving?[12]

However long it takes us to forgive, what is clear from the last verse of the story Jesus told is that at some point each of us is able to choose to forgive and that God requires us to do it.

Forgiveness and Prayer

Have you ever noticed that the same points about forgiving others are mentioned in the Lord's Prayer and in the verse that follows it? Jesus told the people to pray like this:

> Our Father in heaven, may your name be
>   kept holy.
> May your Kingdom come soon.
> May your will be done on earth, as it is
>   in heaven.
> Give us today the food we need, and
>   forgive us our sins, *as we have forgiven
>   those who sin against us.*
> And don't let us yield to temptation,
>   but rescue us from the evil one.
> (Matthew 6:9–12 NLT, emphasis added)

The words "as we have forgiven" assume that before we come to God seeking forgiveness for ourselves, we have already forgiven those who have sinned against us. After he shared this prayer, Jesus told those who were listening, "If you forgive those who sin against you, your heavenly Father will forgive you. But if you refuse to forgive others, your Father will not forgive your sins" (verses 14–15).

Why won't God forgive us unless we forgive others?

Did you notice the word *refuse* in the verse above? Refusing to forgive is very different from being willing to forgive but just not yet ready to do it. When a person knows God wants them to forgive, but they choose not to, saying in their heart, "I *refuse* to forgive. I *will not* forgive," their attitude is rebellious rather than submissive toward God. Rebellion toward God interrupts our fellowship with him. If you refuse to forgive—to release another person from the debt they owe you—that unforgiveness puts a barrier between you and God. God will not respond to a request for your own personal forgiveness until you do for the other person what you are asking God to do for you.

Psalm 66:18 says, "If I had not confessed the sin in my heart, the Lord would not have listened" (NLT). But when the Psalmist confessed his wrong attitude to God, the barrier between him and God was removed. As a result, in the next verse he happily reports, "God did listen! He paid attention to my prayer." That's exactly how it works for us. When you forgive the one who has hurt you, that step of obedience shows that the change in your attitude toward God is real. And God responds by forgiving you as you have forgiven the other person.

House Rules

A house rule, according to the Merriam-Webster Dictionary, is "a rule ... that applies only among a certain group or in a certain place." Many parents have established house rules that give their children a clear understanding of what the parents consider to be acceptable behavior. An article titled "A Sample of Family Household Rules" suggests that parents consider making house rules such as:

- Knock on closed doors before entering.

- Make amends when you hurt someone.

- Tell the truth.

- Ask permission to borrow other people's belongings.[13]

House rules set the standards for children's behavior within the family. Rules such as the ones above require children to respect people and property, to show kindness, and to be truthful. In short, house rules help the kids know how to treat their parents and each other.

In the family of God, forgiving others is a house rule. It's how the Father wants his kids to treat each other. As the Author of forgiveness, our Father loves it when his children follow in his footsteps, practicing forgiveness as a way of life. Concerning forgiveness, God asks three things of his children:

GOD'S HOUSE RULES

1 Always forgive others.

2 Ask others to forgive you.

3 Never take revenge.

Let's take a deeper look at each of these.

1. Always forgive others.

My friend David was stunned and heartbroken when his wife, Holly, admitted to unfaithfulness and announced her plan to end their marriage. In the gut-wrenching months that followed, David's world was turned upside down by a one-sided divorce that forever changed his life and the lives of his and Holly's children.

Blindsided by his wife's betrayal and consumed with anger, David struggled with the thought of forgiving Holly. As a Christ follower, he understood the importance of forgiveness, but his many painful and confusing emotions kept him from forgiving Holly. What made the situation even more difficult was, because of their children, he had to interact with Holly often and she was not always cordial.

One day David's feelings about forgiving Holly collided with the words of Jesus in Luke 6:46—"Why do you call me, 'Lord, Lord,' and do not do what I say?" As the words sank into his heart, he knew that the time to forgive Holly had come. He prayed, "God, I'm angry now, but I have the power to forgive through you," and despite his emotions, he chose to forgive Holly.

Since that day, whenever there are difficult moments with Holly, David has continued to practice forgiveness. "What I choose to do," he said, "is just keep going to the Lord, saying, 'I want to forgive her in my heart.'" He readily admits, "It still hurts. Sometimes it's not in my heart to want to forgive," but each time, with God's help, he chooses to forgive again.

One day, Peter, one of Jesus's disciples, came to him and asked, "Lord, how many times shall I forgive my brother or sister who sins against me?" Peter probably thought he was going above and beyond when he suggested, "Up to seven times?" He may have been more than a little surprised to hear Jesus reply, "I tell you, not seven times, but seventy-seven times!" (Matthew 18:21–22).

God does not ask us to forgive others more often than he is willing to forgive us!

2. Ask others to forgive you.

It's impossible for any of us to go through life without stepping on someone else's toes. We're all imperfect; we all make mistakes, and all of us have said and done things along the way that have offended or hurt others. Sometimes we don't realize that we have offended someone. But when we do realize it, the right thing to do, the thing God wants us to do, is humbly ask them to forgive us.

As brothers and sisters in the family of God, our unity matters to our Father. In fact, being in right, authentic relationships with other believers is so important that Jesus gave this instruction to his followers: "If you are offering your gift at the altar and there remember that your brother or sister has something against you, leave your gift there in front of the altar. First go and be reconciled to them; then come and offer your gift" (Matthew 5:23–24). To say that another way, if we know we have hurt or offended another believer, God doesn't even want our gifts until we have asked that person to forgive us and made an effort to reconcile with them.

Forgiveness is essential to maintaining the unity God wants his children to have. When you're the one who needs to be forgiven, it's humbling, and maybe a bit intimidating too, to ask for forgiveness. But it's always the right thing to do. If that person is willing to forgive you, it may be possible to also restore your relationship with them. But even if they are unwilling to forgive you, you've still done the right thing by reaching out and asking for forgiveness. By seeking reconciliation, you have followed Paul's counsel: "If it is possible, *as far as it depends on you,* live at peace with everyone" (Romans 12:18, emphasis added). You can always feel good about asking someone to forgive you, regardless of the outcome.

When someone cares enough to ask another person to forgive them, it can have a profound and positive impact on that person. My friend Kara can attest to this. Like David, she was blindsided by a divorce she never saw coming. After her husband left, several of Kara's friends surrounded her in support, but one of her closer friends just quietly stepped away. This friend never said anything unkind to Kara, and there was no issue between them. So Kara was puzzled when, without explanation, this friend just gradually disappeared from her life. Kara sensed that the woman no longer wanted to be associated with her simply because she was now divorced. Kara felt rejected and sad. Since she hadn't wanted the divorce, losing a friend because of it seemed painfully unfair. As time went on, whenever the two women crossed paths they would pause to say a friendly hello, but not much more. These casual encounters made Kara's heart ache, and they never really reconnected as friends.

> You can always feel good about asking someone to forgive you, regardless of the outcome.

One day more than ten years later, Kara was surprised to get a phone call from her former friend. As the conversation turned to the past. Kara could tell that the woman was speaking from her heart with sincere regret when she admitted, "I didn't treat you right." She asked Kara to forgive her. Kara's *yes* was immediate. She felt relieved and joyful. Looking back on that conversation now, Kara says, "That phone call meant so much to me. I know it must have taken courage for her to reach out to me after such a long time. Her humility and sincerity really touched my heart. If I ever need to ask someone to forgive me, that phone call will be my model for how to do it."

3. Never take revenge.

As my friend David discovered, forgiving others is often complicated by the emotional pain we experience when someone sins against us. It hurts to be bullied, treated dismissively, gossiped about, yelled at, shunned, or treated poorly in any other way. Whether your pain is physical, emotional, or both, one thing God will never guide you to do is pay someone back for what they did to you. God's direction on this is clear in both the Old and New Testaments:

> Do not seek revenge or bear a grudge against anyone among your people but love your neighbor as yourself. I am the LORD.
>
> LEVITICUS 19:18

> It is mine to avenge; I will repay.
>
> DEUTERONOMY 32:35

> Dear friends, never take revenge. Leave that to the righteous anger of God. For the Scriptures say, "I will take revenge; I will pay them back," says the Lord.
>
> ROMANS 12:19 NLT

Payback is not our job; it's God's job. He has promised, "I will repay," and God keeps his promises. You can trust that he will work in the other person's life in exactly the right way and at exactly the right time.

Chapter 2
Real-World Forgiveness

SEVERAL YEARS AGO, A FRIEND INVITED ME AND MY son to join her family for a few days at the beach in the Outer Banks of North Carolina. So we made the trip! The weather was beautiful, and we all spent many hours enjoying the beach and exploring the area. When our beach vacation came to an end, my son and I took our time driving home, stopping to visit some interesting places, like the Wright Brothers National Memorial.

I had planned carefully for the trip, and I thought I knew exactly how much money I had spent at the beach. But when I opened my wallet to pay for the admission tickets at our first stop, I was taken aback.

What had I forgotten to account for? I couldn't think of anything. So the missing money remained a mystery—until one day about a year later when my friend called and asked an unexpected question. She said, "When you got home from the beach, were you missing any money?" I said yes. She explained that she had found money stashed in an unusual place in her daughter's room. Putting the pieces together, she realized that the money had to be mine and she was calling to apologize. Apparently, one afternoon while I was on the beach, her daughter had found my purse and stolen the money.

The phone call left me with a rather unique mixture of emotions. It felt good to finally have an explanation for the missing money. At the same time, I felt violated, knowing that the girl had gone into my room at the beach house, deliberately searched through my purse, and helped herself to the money in my wallet. I was also hurting for my friend because she was grieved and embarrassed about what her daughter had done.

In this swirl of emotions, I remembered something that suddenly filled me with empathy. I recalled that this child had some special issues that her parents and she had been addressing for a long time with mental health counselors. I also knew that her behavior had been disruptive and difficult for the whole family. And now, since this was not the first time the girl had stolen something, my aggrieved friend and her husband were already addressing the issue again with their daughter.

This situation called for my forgiveness. Because I knew the backstory, I could put the theft in the context of that much bigger picture. Knowing the "inside story" triggered the empathy that made it easy to forgive the wrong that had been done.

Empathy and Forgiveness

Forgiveness researchers now know that there is a connection between empathy and forgiveness. A publication by the American Psychological Association states, "True forgiveness offers something positive—empathy, compassion, understanding—to the person who hurt you."[14] Experts in the field of forgiveness research recommend bringing empathy into our thinking about a person who has hurt us. What might that person have been dealing with in their own life that played a role in how they treated you or spoke to you? For example, have they just lost their job? Gone bankrupt? Experienced the death of a close friend or family member? Miscarried a baby? Gone through a divorce? Rethinking some of our offenses in the context of the hurtful person's family problems, job stress, financial difficulties, poor health, or other painful aspects of their personal life may make it easier to sincerely say, "I forgive."

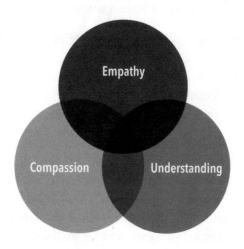

In retrospect, I can now see how empathy played a big part in transforming my initial response to another "forgiveness challenge" that came my way. Here's the story:

For many years, the same reliable accountant had prepared my taxes. Each year, when the taxes were ready, I got a phone call asking me to come sign the forms so she could submit them electronically. One year, I realized that it was getting close to the filing deadline, and I had not received a call to come in and sign the forms. Concerned, I emailed the accountant and inquired about the status of my taxes. When she did not reply to my email or to a voicemail message, I decided to go to the office in person.

I was relieved to find her assistant at the reception desk and I asked her if my taxes were ready. She said they were not. I asked when she thought they might be ready. She said she didn't know. That seemed like an odd answer, since the filing deadline was now just days away. I asked her what was going on.

Sheepishly, she explained that my taxes would not be done by the filing deadline because her boss had gone on vacation. *What?* I was incredulous. She took a vacation during tax season? And she left without doing my taxes and didn't even let me know? Needless to say, I was not a happy camper. If the accountant had just let me know her vacation plans in time, I could have found someone else to do my taxes. Now, I would surely face a penalty for filing late. I had known this very responsible woman for many years, and this behavior was completely out of character.

My taxes were in fact filed late that year and there was in fact a penalty. I still couldn't wrap my head around what had happened, so the next year I found a new tax preparer. It wasn't until a few years had gone by that I learned the explanation for this woman's behavior that had so inconvenienced me. I happened to run into her husband and in that impromptu conversation on the sidewalk, he shared that his wife had dementia. In that moment, I realized that his wife's odd and seemingly uncaring neglect of my taxes had been an early sign of her dementia. Her unprofessional treatment of me (and probably other clients too) was not really "her," but the disease that had begun to take hold of her.

> Rethinking our offenses in the context of the painful aspects of the hurtful person's life may make it easier to say "I forgive."

Understanding the reason for her behavior during that maddening tax filing experience now filled me with empathy. I felt compassion for this woman and also for her husband. And the resentment that had lingered in my heart was transformed into forgiveness.

In both this situation and the earlier one at the beach, the offenses that seemed to be motivated only by selfishness were actually driven by factors the person could not control. Both of these scenarios are a bit unusual, but because this has been my experience twice, I don't want to miss the lesson. This is my takeaway: we should always be empathetic toward those who offend us because so often we just don't know, and may never discover, the factors that motivated them to behave toward us as they did.

Insensitive Offenses

As mentioned in the previous chapter, it's fairly impossible to avoid stepping on other people's toes as we journey through life. We're all imperfect; we've all offended others and we've all been offended by others at times too. Often, when others offend us, it's not because they are malicious; they may just be insensitive. Most insensitive offenses call for the same one-way forgiveness we've focused on so far. Very minor insensitive offenses sometimes call for a somewhat different response.

Here are two stories to help illustrate the difference.

One year when I was in elementary school, my family went through a difficult time. My mother was hospitalized for many months; my little sister went to live with an aunt and uncle in another town, and my father became a temporary single parent, taking care of me. My teacher that year (I'll call her Miss T) was very kind to me, and even invited me to her home. I never forgot her kindness, and when my first book was published many years later, I sent her a copy of the book along with a letter expressing appreciation for her kindness during that difficult time in my young life. Much to my disappointment, I never heard back from Miss T, not even to say thank you for the book. However, I did hear some very unhappy comments from my father.

Miss T, it seems, gave my letter of appreciation to the local newspaper, which published it, apparently along with a story that my father felt reflected poorly on him. The newspaper never contacted me for a comment or to verify the story, so I had no idea this had happened until my father called to express his extreme displeasure at finding information about our family's rough patch in the local paper. I felt truly awful. What I had intended as a kind gesture to Miss T had turned into a disaster! My father was angry with me; I was upset with Miss T for not asking my permission before making my personal letter public, and I was very disappointed that the newspaper had not verified with me what they were about to publish. Yet, with the newspaper now delivered to every front porch in the community, what could I do except profusely apologize to my father?

Here's the second, more recent experience: One Sunday several years ago, as everyone was leaving the worship service, a woman called out to me across the pews. What had I done to my hair, she wanted to know. The color, she proclaimed in the hearing of all, didn't look natural! I don't remember what was going on with my hair that day, but I do remember cringing with embarrassment.

I'm confident that neither Miss T nor my hair critic intended any offense. They were just insensitive to the impact of their words and actions. Perhaps Miss T felt she was rendering community service of some sort by giving the newspaper a "hometown girl makes good" story. It just probably never occurred to her that my father still lived in the same small town, and that he would not appreciate finding my letter in the local paper. Miss T probably also never considered how I would feel, discovering that my letter to her had been made public, but never hearing back from her myself.

How should we respond to insensitive offenses? The answer of course, is that, as with all other offenses, we should forgive them. But when it comes to insensitive offenses, forgiveness can look a little different depending on how deeply we have been affected. Take as examples, the two incidents above. They were, for me, at opposite ends of the impact scale.

While I believe Miss T intended no harm, some harm was done. Her insensitivity impacted me quite a bit. I had to work through what she didn't do (acknowledge my letter and the book), what she did do (made my personal letter public), and I also had to try to soothe my father's anger. My response to this insensitive offense, though it came much later, was to choose to forgive Miss T.

The comment about my hair was at the opposite end of the impact scale. It was a slight offense, so it only had a slight impact on me. While the woman's insensitivity did create an uncomfortable moment for me, in the grand scheme of things, it wasn't a big deal.

When an offense is slight, while we could choose to harbor resentment about it, we could also choose to mirror Proverbs 19:11, which says, "It is to one's glory to overlook an offense." In other words, the recipe for responding to a slightly insensitive offense can simply be, with grace and a dash of empathy, to just let it go. In the words of Lewis Smedes, "Not every hurt needs to be forgiven ... when all we need is simply a little spiritual generosity."[15] After all, as noted above, who among us has not sometimes been insensitive to others? We all need to be good "overlookers," sometimes giving and

> We all sometimes need to be good "overlookers."

sometimes receiving the grace to just let lesser offenses go. It is, as the proverb says, "to one's glory" to do so.

Anonymous Offenses

Perhaps the most difficult forgiveness challenges many of us will ever face are offenses that are done to us deliberately, but anonymously. The offenses I have in mind were not even possible a few decades ago. They are possible now because of the rapid advances in technology that have made home delivery services so tremendously convenient. These helpful services become terrible headaches, however, when unscrupulous people use them to take deliberate advantage of others—while remaining completely, frustratingly, anonymous.

Here's one anonymous offense that happened to me:

One day I received a text that said my groceries were ready for pickup. I had ordered groceries online from this national chain store several times before and had received a text just like this each time. What was concerning was that I had not ordered any groceries from this store recently. When I took a closer look at the text, I became alarmed. The groceries were indeed ready for pickup—*in California*. I live in North Carolina.

I quickly realized that somehow my store account, linked to both my credit card number and my contact information, had fallen into the hands of a complete stranger two thousand miles across the country. And the fact that the groceries were now on their way out the door might mean they were already paid for. I called the store and spoke to a man who took immediate action on my behalf. He canceled the grocery order. I also quickly canceled my account with the store and notified my bank.

I had so many questions! How had this happened? Was this the only account that was in jeopardy? Or was this just the beginning of a bigger problem? And who could this anonymous thief be? I felt helpless, vulnerable, and violated.

Another time, the deliberate but anonymous actions of another person left me feeling much the same way, but for different reasons. Here's what happened that time:

A few days before Christmas, I arrived home to find that a large box had been delivered to our front porch. My sister and I had agreed to exchange Christmas gifts this way, so I had been expecting this package. But as soon as I looked at the address label I knew something was wrong. My name was misspelled and that was not a mistake my sister would make.

I brought the box inside and opened it. Peering inside, I saw several gifts wrapped in Christmas paper. Some of the wrapping paper was torn and some of the name tags were askew. One gift was missing half its paper entirely (pajamas for me—one surprise spoiled). As I lifted the gifts from the box, I discovered a note from the delivery service. It was a mass-produced official apology note. It explained that in order to ship so many packages quickly, sometimes accidents happen, and they are sorry. Hmmm. Okay, I understood. A few messier-than-normal packages, but no real harm done.

I put the packages under the Christmas tree and called my sister to let her know the box had arrived. She reminded me to put the tin of her homemade pecan tarts (one of my son's favorites) in the refrigerator. Uh-oh. It dawned on me that I had not seen the annual tin of treats. I reviewed the packages. Nope, no cookie tin. My sister asked me to count the presents and she said the number seemed right. So we surmised that the original shipping box must have gotten caught in a machine or been run over by a truck, and the cookie tin must not have survived the accident. Just one of those things, we agreed.

I forgot about all of this until Christmas morning. My sister had sent two gifts for my son in addition to the unfortunate cookie tin. One was in a small gold box. The sides were not taped, so my son simply lifted the lid. A Starbucks gift card holder! My son was very pleased ... until he lifted the flap. There was no gift card.

The damaged box theory suddenly seemed a lot less likely. While I was willing to concede that the cookie tin may have been crushed and the contents rendered inedible, there was no getting around the fact that the gift card had been deliberately removed. Someone lifted the lid on the little gold box just as my son did, felt pleasure at seeing the Starbucks gift card holder, just as my son did, and then took the gift card for themselves. Now I wondered, had the cookie tin really been damaged, or had the goodies just been too yummy-looking to resist? At any rate, two of the three gifts my sister had given her only nephew for Christmas were gone. We all felt sad.

Even though the examples above deal with theft, deliberate anonymous offenses aren't limited to stealing. Some people have made the unhappy discovery that while they were shopping or at work, someone hit their parked car and didn't leave a note. Some homeowners have stepped onto their deck with their morning coffee in hand only to find that someone spray painted their garage doors with racial slurs or profanity during the night. Still others have cowered in terror in their own home as it is being hit with bullets in a drive-by shooting. In any of these anonymous and highly offensive situations, who wouldn't feel indignation?

Anonymous offenses challenge our resolve to forgive in ways that other kinds of offenses don't. When wrongs are done to us anonymously, there is an added sense of outrage that the person "got away with it" because they cannot be identified. Forgiving the nameless, faceless person responsible, whoever and wherever they may be,

> Choosing to forgive can help restore your sense of control and let you feel like a victor rather than a victim.

won't undo the harm that was done to you. But as you regain your composure and reflect on the incident, choosing to forgive can help restore your sense of control and let you feel like a victor rather than a victim. When there's no one to hold accountable, *take care of yourself* by forgiving. And remember this: the responsible person isn't anonymous to God. He knows who they are, and he will deal with them in time, and in exactly the right way. Meanwhile, they're on your mind now, so as you strive to think of them with empathy, also pray for them. God has a plan for their lives too.

Heroic Forgiveness

Even when the balm of empathy has softened the heart of an offended person, for many, the choice to forgive still often comes far more from the will than from the emotions. This is never more true than for those who choose to respond to life-altering offenses with what some call *heroic forgiveness*.

Life-altering offenses are those that take from a person something they can never get back. Sometimes it's not another individual but a government mandate that inflicts an unrecoverable, life-altering offense. One example of this began in the early 1900s when thousands of people in thirty-three US states were involuntarily sterilized. State governments rationalized that this practice, called eugenics, would improve the genetic composition of society by preventing people with "undesirable" qualities from having children. Those who were forced to undergo sterilization were mostly those with mental health issues, poor or on welfare, disabled, sick, undereducated, imprisoned, or in someone's opinion, promiscuous, feeble-minded, or lazy. In California, about 20,000 people were involuntarily sterilized. In North Carolina, where I live, between 1929 and 1974 more than 7,500 people, some as young as age ten, were involuntarily, sometimes unknowingly, sterilized. Most were women.[16] Thousands of these people are still alive today, still grieving the fact that their ability to have children was so unfairly taken away from them. Forgiving that kind of permanent, life-altering offense requires nothing short of heroic forgiveness.

Marci's Story

My friend Marci experienced a life-altering loss of a different sort. One day when she was at work, she got a phone call that began what would become for her and her family a heart-rending ordeal. She was horrified to learn that her mother had been brutally murdered in her own home. Who would do such a thing to someone as kind and wonderful as her mother? And why? Marci remembers, "It was so traumatic that I was literally shaking."

The day before the funeral, Marci learned that the murderer was a man who had been renting her mom's upstairs apartment. When she heard the gruesome details of what her mom had suffered, shocked to her core and in terrible anguish, Marci's only thought was revenge. She recalls:

> We had been at the funeral home finalizing the arrangements for the funeral. When I heard what had taken place, I was so angry. I walked outside and I slammed one fist so hard against the other that my ring finger started to bleed. At that moment, what popped into my head was, "Vengeance is mine, I will repay, says the Lord." My parents were strong Christians and they had instilled that verse in me from a very young age. I knew revenge was not the right way to go. But I was not in a forgiveness state of mind. This was the loss of a person who meant everything to me. I was too impacted by the loss, the trauma, and the shock to forgive.

Many years passed before Marci finally forgave her mother's killer. Reflecting on her very long journey to forgiveness, she said:

If someone is really part of your inner circle, that loss is traumatic, and that trauma takes time to process. Sin is sin, but there is a difference between somebody stealing a pack of gum from you and murdering your loved one. Some things can easily be forgiven and recovered from, but when you lose someone that is so dear to you in such a brutal and sudden way, that takes a different level of forgiveness. I had to get through years of the anniversary of her death, her birthday, Christmas, Mother's Day, and other times that I would want to be sharing with her. It was all taken away. I had to process that … and it was very difficult.

Those of us who have had only lesser offenses to forgive may have trouble understanding how it could take years for Marci to arrive at forgiveness. We might even tend to judge her, thinking we would surely have forgiven much quicker. But forgiving something as difficult as the brutal murder of a loved one is much more emotionally complex than anything most of us have experienced. It truly is *heroic* forgiveness. Here's why:

After a terrible trauma, a person may feel overwhelmed by devastating emotions. The emotional pain is even worse if the person believes they are supposed to "forgive and forget." The problem with "forgive and forget" is ... we can't forget! We don't have the ability to erase the memory of an experience we'd rather forget. God alone is able to "forgive and forget." In both the Old and New Testaments, we read God's promise to forget the sins he forgives us for: "I will never again remember their sins" (Jeremiah 31:34; also Hebrews 10:17).

Unlike God, we can't just decide to "never again remember" something. While some of our memories may diminish over time, it is very unlikely that the memory of a truly horrific experience will ever completely disappear. That's because we have a brain structure, the amygdala, that actually keeps us from forgetting our most emotionally intense experiences. God has lovingly wired us this way for our own protection. Remembering things that are painful and dangerous helps us survive. But this inability to forget our greatest hurts can be a huge obstacle to forgiving someone. Painful memories, coupled with the myth of "forgive and forget," can trap people in unforgiveness. Some people may believe that if you can't forget what happened, you haven't really forgiven it. Others may believe that if you're able to "forgive and forget," it means you really didn't care that much anyway. This was the sticking point for Marci.

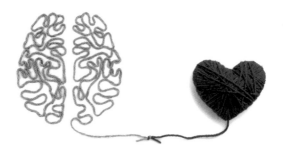

Whenever Marci thought about the gruesome details of her mother's murder, she imagined the physical and emotional pain her mother must have endured as she was being viciously beaten and stabbed to death. These thoughts triggered devastating emotions for Marci that made her freeze at the thought of forgiveness. She was fighting a difficult and ironic emotional battle. Because of the Christian truths that Marci's mom had instilled in her, Marci not only knew that God wanted her to forgive, but that her mother would also now want her to forgive what had been done. But because of the "forgive and forget" myth, Marci believed that forgiving the killer would be like saying she didn't really care that much about her mother's suffering. And so the memories of what happened to her mom were at the same time both breaking her heart and keeping her stuck in unforgiveness.

I asked Marci, "So, how were you finally able to forgive?"

She said, "I think everybody has their own inner dialogue with the Lord, and God knows exactly how we feel. Even though others might not totally comprehend, it was just deeply intimate and personal, and God understood me. I knew that it hurts yourself to harbor resentment. I knew that forgiveness was right, and I knew that I needed to forgive this person. But I was hanging on because of pain. The Lord had to help me separate forgiveness from the strong feelings of loss. It was my ongoing prayer, asking the Lord to help me separate forgiveness from the thought that forgiving would mean that I loved my mother less. And I just had to keep praying. I needed reassurance from the Lord that I wasn't dishonoring the memory of my mother by forgiving this person.

> "The Lord had to help me separate forgiveness from the strong feelings of loss. It was my ongoing prayer."
>
> MARCI

"Even though I knew I needed to forgive, there was a part of me that didn't want to. My prayers were sort of like this: 'You know, Father, this is really hard for me. If I forgive this person it feels like I'm diminishing the value of my mother to me.' And God would put thoughts in my mind, to basically say, 'What I'm asking you is different. I'm not asking you to love your mother any less. I'm just saying that you need to give this person grace. And to forgive them, regardless of what their deed was, because it is what I ask you to do. And it's what I do for you.'

"Each time this occurred, I would raise a defense. Until one day my prayers and God's response took hold. And I untied the connection between forgiveness and dishonoring my mother. I remembered how Jesus was willing to forgive us even though mankind took his life. And those thoughts laid the foundation for forgiveness. It was a process, but I finally got to the point that I could truly forgive. And when I did that, I felt a burden lifted off me because I felt that this was what God wanted me to do. The sorrow is still in my heart, but I'm happy to say, so is forgiveness."

The Two Sides of Forgiveness

Experts know that forgiveness has both a decisional and an emotional component. This can be seen in Marci's long journey to forgiveness. She knew that she needed to forgive the man who killed her mother. She wanted to do it, and she eventually did, but only after working through her many painful emotions. Dr. Tyler VanderWeele explains this kind of struggle saying that decisional forgiveness is "often quicker and easier to accomplish" but "emotional forgiveness is much harder and takes longer." This is because of the negative feelings that reoccur "when something triggers the memory, or you still suffer from the adverse consequences of the action."[17]

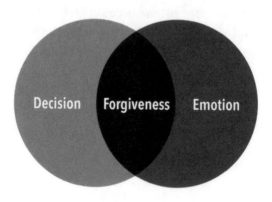

Emotional forgiveness may be most elusive when a situation that calls for heroic forgiveness "triggers the memory" in an ongoing way. As Marci mentioned, for many years, every Mother's Day was a painful reminder of her mom's murder that made it harder for her to forgive. For the men and women who were involuntarily sterilized, Mother's Day or Father's Day is an annual reminder that they will never be moms or dads.

While most divorces don't call for heroic forgiveness, their impact is often ongoing, sometimes in ways that catch people off guard. For example, David once found himself seated at the same (thankfully large) restaurant table as the man who had broken up his marriage to Holly. Similarly, Kara was glad that her ex came to celebrate their daughter's birthday, but she had not expected him to bring his new girlfriend to the party. In awkward social situations like these, unresolved resentment and bitterness only add more weight to the emotional stress; those negative emotions are part of the heavy cargo of unforgiveness that God wants us to jettison from our lives.

Forgiveness as a Way of Life

As you recall, forgiveness is *unilateral* when it only involves the person who was offended. (*Uni* comes from a Latin word that means "one.") Unilateral forgiveness is an offended person's private, inner decision to release toxic bitterness, resentment, or the desire for revenge. It's the decision to no longer hold a person's wrongs against them. In his World Day of Peace message in 2002, Pope John Paul II provided the world with a "gold standard" definition for forgiveness. He said, "Forgiveness is above all a personal choice, a decision of the heart to go against the natural instinct to pay back evil with evil."

> "Forgiveness is above all a personal choice, a decision of the heart to go against the natural instinct to pay back evil with evil."
>
> POPE JOHN PAUL II

Because unilateral forgiveness requires nothing from the person who caused the offense, it doesn't matter if that other person has asked for your forgiveness or not. It doesn't matter if they have no remorse for what they did. It doesn't matter if they're not speaking to you or if their deeds were done to you anonymously. It doesn't even matter if the person has died. You can still forgive them—because the purpose of forgiving is to set yourself free.

When we finally come to understand that forgiving others is for our own benefit, and that God is pleased when we forgive as we have been forgiven, we no longer want to harbor the ugly fruits of unforgiveness. And so, in the perfect providence of God, we may sometimes be given unique, even personalized, opportunities to forgive others. These forgiveness opportunities come to us uninvited, disguised as offenses that test our willingness to forgive. As we navigate these forgiveness challenges one by one, though we may not even realize it, we are slowly embracing forgiveness as our way of life.

Forgiving the Past Moves You Forward

Unless we were taught during childhood to forgive others, by the time we learn the importance of forgiveness in our adult years, many of us have accumulated a lifelong backlog of unforgiven incidents. As we begin to forgive the words and actions of others in the present, long-forgotten wounds from the distant past may begin to surface. We may then realize that some of our current issues are actually rooted in things that happened when we were very young. As children, we may have simply buried in our hearts the painful incidents we didn't know how to deal with.

Living with unforgiveness is stressful. One research study found that "people who had greater levels of accumulated lifetime stress exhibited worse mental health outcomes," but for those who "scored high on measures of forgiveness, high lifetime stress didn't predict poor mental health."[18] These findings affirm the positive mental health effects of forgiving others. For many of us, looking backward in time to forgive may be what we need do in order to move forward in freedom.

On a personal note, as I have given so much thought to forgiveness while writing this book, memories of unforgiven, long-forgotten incidents have come to mind. Some are from my childhood and teenage years, some from my college days, and some from the years since college. One by one, as each situation has come to mind, I have not reburied it, but have instead paused to revisit the situation and forgive the person involved. Retrospective forgiveness, I'm finding, is a practical and beautiful thing. It's the only way to bring closure to situations that involve people who have passed away or to begin healing from old memories that are still painful.

> Looking backward in time to forgive may be what we need do in order to move forward in freedom.

Forgiving Yourself

As you look back over your life, you might be surprised, as I was, to realize that there is someone in need of your forgiveness that you've never even thought about forgiving. It's the person you see in the mirror every day. The person who needs your forgiveness most of all may be you.

Forgiving yourself is not the same as excusing yourself. Excusing yourself means mentally rehearsing all the reasons why what you did or didn't do was entirely reasonable, or completely unavoidable, or perfectly justifiable, perhaps because of what someone else did or said. Forgiving yourself means two things:

- Rather than excusing yourself, you now take responsibility for the wrong thing that needs to be forgiven.

- You stop holding that wrong thing against yourself—because it's forgiven!

You are as deserving of your own forgiveness as anyone you have ever forgiven or ever will forgive. Forgive yourself for things you did but shouldn't have done, things you should have done but did not do, what you said but shouldn't have, or failed to say when you should have spoken up. If any or all of those things need God's forgiveness as well as yours, admit them as freely to God as you admit them to yourself. Ask for and accept his forgiveness and then forgive yourself as freely and fully as God has forgiven you.

> The person who needs your forgiveness most of all may be you.

Self-forgiveness is the ultimate unilateral forgiveness. You are the only person involved, and you are both the forgiver and the one who is forgiven.

When you choose to forgive yourself, you take the toxins of self-blame and self-resentment off life support. When you do that, you begin to reap the same mental, physical, relational, and spiritual benefits that accrue when you forgive another person. Research has revealed that "self-forgiveness is associated

A forgiving heart is aligned with the heart of God.

with both mental and physical health." In a statistical analysis of data from studies that involved almost 18,000 participants, researchers found "a robust correlation between self-forgiveness and psychological well-being." A similar analysis of studies that involved 5,600 people found that "self-forgiveness predicts physical outcomes" as well.[19]

Forgiving yourself just might lead to:

- more enjoyment of the present because you're no longer consumed with the past;

- better relationships as self-focused anger and bitterness fade away;

- less depression, irritability, and anxiety;

- the sense that your life is now more in sync with your faith; and

- the humility to seek the forgiveness of anyone harmed or hurt by the thing you have taken responsibility for and forgiven yourself for.

A forgiving heart is aligned with the heart of God. In light of God's great love and mercy toward you, there is no reason to continue being hard on yourself. And when you make the choice to no longer hold your own wrongs against yourself, the prisoner you've been keeping—that person in the mirror—is set free.

> The LORD is compassionate and gracious,
> slow to anger, abounding in love.
> He will not always accuse,
> nor will he harbor his anger forever;
> he does not treat us as our sins deserve
> or repay us according to our iniquities.
> For as high as the heavens are above the earth,
> so great is his love for those who fear him;
> as far as the east is from the west, so far has he
> removed our transgressions from us.
>
> PSALM 103:8–12

Chapter 3

Forgiveness, Reconciliation, and Trust

"Will you please forgive me?"

Those humble words, sincerely spoken, will sometimes touch the heart of an offended person and open the door to reconciliation. Other times, it is the offended person who reaches out to offer forgiveness to the one who offended them. No matter which person starts the process, the end result can be the restoration of a broken relationship. This is *transactional forgiveness,* the other kind of forgiveness mentioned only briefly in the first chapter.

Unlike unilateral forgiveness, which is *intra*personal, taking place within only one person, transactional forgiveness is *inter*personal, involving both the offended person and the offending person. This kind of forgiveness can only take place if each person is willing to talk with the other. It's transactional because the person who was offended and the person who caused the offense are now interacting or "transacting" with each other. Transactional forgiveness involves one person's repentance and request for forgiveness and the other person's choice to forgive. Psychologist Dr. Ryan Howes has said, "Reconciliation is an interpersonal process where you dialogue with the offender about what happened, exchange stories, express the hurt, listen for the remorse, and begin to reestablish trust. It's a much more complicated, involved process that includes, but moves beyond forgiveness. Forgiveness is solo, reconciliation is a joint venture."[20]

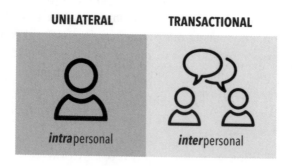

UNILATERAL

TRANSACTIONAL

*intra*personal

*inter*personal

When an offended person forgives the one who caused their hurt, sometimes the misery of estrangement can turn into the joy of restored unity. David wrote in Psalm 133:1, "How good and pleasant it is when God's people live together in unity!" Unity of believers is not only pleasant to those who have reconciled, but also to those who observe the mended relationship. Jesus prayed for his followers, including all of us:

> When estranged believers reconcile, their reunion is a living example of the reconciling love of God.

> May they experience such perfect unity
> that the world will know that
> you sent me and that you love them
> as much as you love me.
>
> JOHN 17:23 NLT

When estranged believers reconcile, their reunion is a living example of the reconciling love of God. Thus, the forgiveness that restores unity is not about getting people to "play nice" with one another so the world will be a better place (although it certainly helps!). Rather, it's about living the way God actually wants us, his children, to live in this broken world.

Transactional Forgiveness

When Jesus gave his life to redeem humanity, he paid for the sins of the whole world. That atonement is meant for all of us, and we're all loved by God. Yet not everyone is forgiven and restored to God. Are you thinking, "*Wait.* If Jesus died for all sin and we're all loved, then why isn't everyone forgiven and restored to God?"

Think of a relationship with God in the same way you think about human relationships. There must be reciprocity. You can't be friends with someone who doesn't want to be friends with you. You can't marry someone who doesn't want to marry you. So even though God has already forgiven everyone, until there is reciprocity—until a person actually accepts the forgiveness that God holds out to them—it goes unclaimed. But when a person says *yes* to God's forgiveness, there is reciprocity, and that person is now restored to God. This transacting of forgiveness between God and humanity is the ultimate example of transactional forgiveness.

It works the same way between people, too. For reconciliation to occur, there must be reciprocity. Both people have to participate, one seeking forgiveness and the other granting it. And very often, when relationships have unraveled *both* people need to seek forgiveness and also grant it to each other.

When Forgiveness Is Refused

When a relationship is restored through transactional forgiveness, it is a beautiful thing. "The miracle of forgiveness is completed," Lewis Smedes observed, "when two alienated people start over again.... It is the beginning of a new journey together."[21] Restoration is the best of all possible outcomes. But unfortunately, restoration is not always what happens. When one person offers forgiveness, it doesn't always pave the way to reconciliation because it takes two to reconcile. If one person offers forgiveness and the other person refuses it, their relationship remains broken. The truth is, just as extending forgiveness is a choice, so is refusing it. So just as some people reject God's forgiveness, some people may reject your forgiveness too.

As noted above, whether you are the hurt person or the person who caused the hurt, when it's safe to do so, it's always right for you to take the initiative in pursuing reconciliation. When you are the person who has been hurt, you have a responsibility, in fact, to reach out to the person who offended you. Matthew 18:15 instructs, "If another believer sins against you, go privately and point out the offense. If the other person listens and confesses it, you have won that person back" (NLT).

If you reach out with forgiveness to a person who has wronged you, and they respond with a laugh, saying they've done nothing wrong, then what? What if they essentially throw your forgiveness in your face and keep walking? The next two verses in Matthew 18 show how deeply God desires unity to be restored between his children. They outline what to do next if the person who wronged you doesn't admit to it: "But if he refuses to listen, then go to him again and take one or two other people with you.... If he refuses to listen to them, then tell it to the church. If he refuses to listen to the church, then treat him as you would one who does not believe in God" (Matthew 18:16–17 ICB).

In its own way, the rejection of your kindness is another offense, an added hurt. One more thing to forgive. If someone rejects the olive branch you hold out to them, it may make you want to forget about forgiveness. But remember what Jesus said? "If you refuse to forgive others, your Father will not forgive your sins" (Matthew 6:15 NLT). There's nothing in that verse about whether the other person wants to be forgiven. It's about your one-way forgiveness, not about reconciling with the other person. Just as God's forgiveness won't mean much to a person who doesn't want to accept it, neither will yours. You must still forgive them, no longer in hopes of reconciliation, but just because it's what God asks you to do—for your own peace of mind and well-being. And then, do as Jesus did when people rejected him: don't chase after them. Let them go. Leave your forgiveness "on the table," so to speak, just as God does for those who may one day have a change of heart.

> "The miracle of forgiveness is completed when two alienated people start over again."
> LEWIS SMEDES

When Forgiveness Is Withheld

Since we all tromp on each other's toes from time to time as we journey through life, sometimes you're the person who needs to be forgiven. So you ask the person you offended to forgive you. But what if that brother or sister chooses to ignore the Father's "house rule" about forgiveness? What if they choose to instead lock the door to reconciliation?

Here's my story about an experience like that:

My friend Kellie and I were part of a group that had been meeting one evening each week to discuss a topic we were all interested in. Both Kellie and I had some responsibilities in the group. One evening, I chose to attend the meeting even though I was on the verge of exhaustion, both physically and mentally. By the end of the meeting I was really struggling to stay afloat, depleted to the point of just shutting down. I barely had the energy to speak. Not surprisingly, I failed to communicate well with Kellie about our after-meeting tasks. And also not surprisingly, Kellie didn't understand what was going on with me and in that moment I couldn't muster the energy to explain. In hindsight, I knew that I had made the wrong decision. I should have skipped the meeting and instead gone straight to bed after work.

On the drive home, I worried that, without meaning to, I had offended Kellie. When I got home, with all the energy I could summon, I emailed a brief apology to her before crawling into bed:

> Kellie, I am sorry that I did not have the emotional energy to engage you in conversation. I am thinking I should call you and say this, but I still just cannot speak right now. So I am writing this email instead. Please forgive me, and even though you don't understand me right now, I hope you will give me grace. Undeserved, of course. I cherish your friendship, Kellie, even though right now I can't do any better than this note to demonstrate that.

Unfortunately, my weary actions had spoken much louder to Kellie than my emailed apology did. When she and I met up in person a few days later, she told me I was self-centered and that all she had seen in the email was the word *I*. My response only offended her more and she decided on the spot to end our friendship. I was stunned.

Soon after that meeting, I sat down and wrote her a heartfelt letter, hoping to repair the damage and hoping for forgiveness. She did not respond. A few weeks later, I mailed a second letter, written by hand

and tied with a ribbon. Weeks turned into months. I reached out again with a brief email. Then I sent her a birthday card. Again, no response. I finally faced the fact that she did not want to rekindle our friendship. I sent her one last note that said, in part:

> Sometimes God brings a person across our path for just a certain season of life.... I am okay with the idea that this season is now past, and that you need to put some distance between us.... I understand that sometimes this is best for one or both of the people. If this is what you want to/ need to do ... accepted and understood.... Love you, Kellie.

I hoped she would respond to this final note, but she did not.

At that point I decided to accept her decision, knowing that I had reached out multiple times and that the ball was now squarely in her court. And for a long time, I was okay with it. I moved on and thought less and less about Kellie. Then, one morning I woke up at 2:00 a.m. and started thinking. I realized that I was really *not* so okay with it. I began to feel the pain of forgiveness withheld. As I lay there in the darkness, I wondered if withholding forgiveness gives a person a sense of power. Or a feeling of control over the other person. I thought about the Matthew 18 passage where Peter comes to Jesus and says, "Lord, how often shall my brother sin against me and I forgive him? Up to seven times?" Jesus says, "I do not say to you, up to seven times, but up to seventy times seven." I was hurting. I wanted to be forgiven. I *needed* to be forgiven! My heart ached because the connection between my friend and me had been broken—and it was because I had offended her. By 5:00 a.m. I was wondering about something else. I wondered if part of the reason Jesus wants us to forgive each other is because he knows how bad it feels when forgiveness is withheld.

As the months went on, knowing that Kellie was a Christ follower, I became concerned about her in a different way. I thought about the verses that come right after the Lord's Prayer: "If you forgive those who sin against you, your heavenly Father will forgive you. But if you refuse to forgive others, your Father will not forgive your sins." I was concerned now not only about the demise of our friendship, but also about her connection with God. From that point on, my only action was to pray for Kellie. Whenever she came to mind, I simply asked God to work in her heart and move her to forgive me.

Then one day, exactly two years, two months, and twenty-one days from our original misunderstanding—on the day before my birthday—I got an email from Kellie. It said:

> I hope you are well and hope you have a very blessed birthday tomorrow! Would you be willing to get together and talk? I sincerely want to apologize for my hurtful words and behaviors and to ask your forgiveness and I would like to do that in person.

Of course I said yes. We met up at a restaurant a few days later. We had a friendly conversation that got us caught up on each other's lives, and in the course of that conversation we finally reconciled with one another. We did not stay in touch after that meeting, but I was, and still am, fine with that. In the more than two years since we had last spoken, our lives had gone in different directions. It was enough that we had closed the loop with mutual forgiveness.

One of the most interesting aspects of this long journey to our reconciliation is how Kellie's angry "I refuse to forgive you" silence became, in the end, a sincere "please forgive me" request. Our relational disconnect had started out as a one-way offense. By the time we finally reconciled it had grown into a two-way offense. That is, because Kellie ignored sincere requests for forgiveness for more than two years, she eventually felt the need to ask me to forgive her too.

Long after Kellie and I reconciled, I learned about the importance of bringing empathy into the forgiveness process. In retrospect, I now wonder if we might have reconciled sooner if I had given more empathetic thought to a serious trauma Kellie had experienced years before I knew her. Maybe greater empathy on my part would have helped reopen her heart toward me sooner.

Forgiving When You Can't Forget

Marci, who struggled for so long to forgive the man who murdered her mother, can now speak from experience about how good it feels to finally forgive. She said, "Once you forgive, you will lose the anger and resentment for the person that committed the act." But for as long as you delay forgiving, she cautions, "You are consuming your life with something that is not going to make you happy."

Marci is right: unforgiveness does indeed sabotage happiness. While an offended person may spend a sunny Saturday afternoon angrily rehearsing the wrong that was done to them, the person who caused their pain may be out having loads of fun, completely oblivious to the thought-daggers being sent their way. Whether that person is actually happy or not, the point is that by harboring resentment toward them, the offended person may be creating a deeper misery for themselves than the offense itself created. The only way out of the emotional misery pit, and the only sure path back to happiness, is forgiveness. But as so many of us know from our own experience, untangling ourselves from the emotional tentacles of an offense is often easier said than done. We'd like to climb out of the misery pit, but how? How do we shake ourselves free from the pain of what was done to us?

As mentioned in the previous chapter, we cannot just make ourselves forget something. The human mind doesn't work like that, thanks to the amygdala. The amygdala is a pair of structures in the brain that actually keep us from forgetting the traumatic experiences we'd most like to forget. They are small, almond-shaped, and nestled in the temporal lobes of the brain, behind the temples and nearly level with the eyes. There is one on each side of the brain, and if they're doing a good job, the more emotional angst an experience causes us, the more likely it is that we will remember it. Jon T. Willie, a neurosurgeon at Emory University, explains, "If you have an emotional experience, the amygdala seems to tag that memory in such a way so that it is better remembered."[22] This may explain why emotional forgiveness often comes later than the decision to forgive. When something triggers the memory of an offense, that memory can rekindle the painful emotions that were experienced during the offense. Those emotions can create a powerful barrier to forgiveness, even when a person has already decided that they want to forgive, as was the case with Marci.

In time, most memories do fade to varying degrees, according to research. Other memories, "such as the birth of a child or the cascade of events in a car crash, remain crystal clear, even years later."[23] The reason those strongest memories endure is simple biology: it is the amygdala's job to ensure that your most emotion-generating offenses are not forgotten. Which memories will fade and when or how much they will fade isn't under your control. That's why it's a mistake to wait for your emotions to give you the green light to forgive. But memories of an offense and the difficult emotions that go along with it don't have to keep you from acting on your decision to forgive! Though strong emotions do make it harder to forgive, ultimately, *forgiveness is a decision of the will, not the emotions*. And, sooner or later, we must

> Whenever you become willing to forgive, God will enable you to do it.

forgive because it's what God requires his children to do—house rule, remember? You can be sure of this: whenever you become willing to forgive, God will enable you to do it, whether your emotions are fully in sync with that decision or not.

A New Way to Remember

When you have forgiven a wrong, but painful memories still reoccur from time to time, does this mean you haven't really forgiven? No, it does not. Since our brains are wired to preserve the memory of emotionally traumatic events, we can abandon the "forgive and forget" myth. Do not be surprised that you still remember wrongs you have forgiven or if those memories still trigger your emotions. Those things don't mean you haven't forgiven—they just mean your memory is working!

Lewis Smedes, whose work set forgiveness research in motion, said that "forgiving what we cannot forget creates a new way to remember."[24] Other experts in the field of forgiveness research agree. Dr. Tyler VanderWeele says that remembering our hurts differently is "about changing your reaction to those memories."[25] In other words, after you've forgiven an offense, you can change the way the memory of it impacts your life. If you think differently about what happened to you, you "recycle" the memory in a way that serves a new and different purpose in your life. When we do this, Smedes said, "We change the memory of our past into a hope for our future."[26] Thus, by reframing your memory of an offense, you can transform at least some aspect of it into a blessing for which you can actually be thankful.

Pairing things like forgiveness and blessings with forgiveness of hurtful offenses may seem like a mismatch, until we consider Paul's admonition to "give thanks in all circumstances; for this is God's will for you in Christ Jesus" (1 Thessalonians 5:18). What does Paul mean? The *Asbury Bible Commentary* explains:

> Paul commands his readers to give thanks *in the midst of* all circumstances, not to give thanks *for* all circumstances. There is a world of difference between these two views. The latter denies evil and suffering. The former believes that in every circumstance one can give thanks for hope in Christ that cannot be vanquished.[27]

It is in this sense that thankfulness helps transform the memory of an offense into a blessing. It's a "thank you," not for the wrong that was done, but that God, in his perfect love for you, mysteriously and sovereignly permitted an adversity to touch your life—and as Paul reminds us, "*In all things* God works for the good of those who love him" (Romans 8:28, emphasis added). This is indeed a mysterious, even astonishing promise.

Memories don't go from heartbreaking to "thank you" overnight. Nor will they automatically one day turn into blessings because "time heals all wounds." Grief counselor Worth Kilcrease counters that notion, suggesting that it's not time that heals, but rather what we *do* with our time. His point is that life responds to action, not passive waiting. He explains, "We have to *look* for a new job, *search* for the right house, *study* to get through school. Even if we want to win the lottery, we still have to *buy* the ticket. We have to take the initiative to do something to cause something else to happen."[28]

So before you can respond differently to your memory of an offense, you must first "take the initiative to do something" to change the way you think about it. Here are three ideas that may help you find new ways to remember an offense you can't forget.

1. Find the silver lining.

It's been said that everything that happens to us changes us in some way. It's natural, especially at first, to only notice the negative impact of an offense. But as time goes on, you may discover that there are positive effects too. When the memory of an already-forgiven, but still painful offense comes to mind, look for the silver lining—the positive ways the offense has changed you or your circumstances. For example, do you have more empathy for the struggles of others because of what you have experienced? Have new people come into your life, or have toxic relationships ended, because of the offense? Did you learn anything about yourself as you were pondering forgiveness?

Three more ideas:

- Make a list of things you can choose to be grateful for right now, at this moment in your forgiveness journey.

- Start a "silver lining" list and add to it whenever

you realize another positive result of what happened.

- Journal about your response to the offense or talk about it with a counselor or a friend. Expressing yourself in writing or in conversation may help you recognize positive changes you may not yet have realized.

2. Pray for the one who hurt you.

Whenever a devastating earthquake occurs anywhere on earth, within minutes, even the most obscure village captures the attention of the whole world. Suddenly, people we've never met are "on our radar" and on our hearts. The crisis immediately becomes a magnet that attracts relief organizations from many nations. As volunteers rush in with food, water, blankets, and medical supplies, some also bring the good news of the gospel. People are rescued, both physically in the present and spiritually for eternity. Thus, a natural disaster, something bad, has made many good things also possible.

On a much smaller scale, a similar thing happens when someone seriously offends you. When the offense occurs, it immediately commands your full attention. The person responsible is suddenly on your radar. You may recoil in pain and anger, protesting what was done to you. In that moment, if you bring not just your pain and protest, but also the responsible person, to God in prayer, you release into both the situation and that person's life the supernatural power of God.

And in so doing, even if you don't realize it, you have responded to the biblical mandate to "pray for those who mistreat you" (Luke 6:28). Thus, a wrong done to one of God's children, something bad, has now also accomplished something good.

After you have forgiven, if the one who hurt you stays on your radar because of painful memories, it's possible that your prayer "assignment" for this person may not be over. In the providence of God, you may have crossed paths with them at a pivotal or desperate time in their life. They may have greatly needed, and may still greatly need, your prayers. And though you have forgiven, emotional pain may still make it hard to ask God to bless a person who deeply hurt you. It may be hard to pray good things for someone who sold your child the drug that cost them their life, or the one who broke up your marriage or hurt you in any number of other ways. Yet, your every memory of the

> You are never more like Jesus than when you pray for or show kindness to the one who hurt you.

offense is an opportunity to do as Jesus asked: "Love your enemies and pray for those who persecute you, that you may be children of your Father in heaven" (Matthew 5:44). Jesus is your model for fulfilling this verse. The night before he was crucified, Jesus washed the feet of Judas, knowing what he was about to do. You are never more like Jesus than when you pray for or show kindness to the one who hurt you.

3. Trust that there may be more to your story than you can see.

God's plan for our lives is often much bigger and more amazing than we could ever imagine. There is no better illustration of this than the life of Joseph, found in the book of Genesis, chapters 37–50.

Joseph was greatly loved by his father, Jacob. While Jacob had twelve sons, it was clear to all that Joseph was his favorite. Because of this, Joseph's brothers hated him. Joseph had two dreams about his family bowing down to him, and when he told the dreams to his brothers, they hated him even more. By the time Joseph was seventeen years old, his hateful brothers wanted to kill him, and a terrible wrong was done to Joseph. His brothers threw him into a waterless pit and planned to leave him there to die. But when a caravan of merchants bound for Egypt passed their way, they decided to sell Joseph to them instead. After Joseph was gone, the brothers took a beautiful coat their father had given to Joseph, dipped it in goat blood, and took it back to their father to fake their brother's death.

In Egypt, Joseph was sold again, this time to Potiphar, the captain of Pharaoh's guard. As a slave in Potiphar's house, God caused everything Joseph did to prosper. Potiphar came to respect Joseph's management skills so much that he put him in charge of his entire household and everything he had. But then another terrible wrong was done to Joseph. Potiphar's wife lied and said Joseph had tried to rape her. Joseph, falsely accused, was sent to prison. Once again, through no fault of his own, Joseph now found himself in another pit. But here too, God prospered everything Joseph did. The jailers recognized his talent for administration, and Joseph was put in charge of the whole prison and all the other prisoners.

Sometime later, Pharaoh was desperately seeking someone who could interpret two dreams that were deeply troubling him. When Pharaoh heard that there was a Hebrew man in his prison who had interpreted the dreams of others, he sent for Joseph. He told both dreams to Joseph and God showed Joseph what the dreams meant: Egypt would have seven years of great abundance followed by seven years of severe famine. When Pharaoh discerned that Joseph not only had the wisdom and skill to guide Egypt through what lay ahead, but also a plan to accomplish it, he put Joseph in charge over the whole nation. With that decree, Joseph went from the prison to the palace, and the next step in God's great plan for his life was set in motion.

Pharaoh's dreams came to pass just as God had told Joseph they would. During the years of prosperity, Joseph wisely stored a portion of the nation's crops in preparation for the famine that would come next. When the famine hit, all the nations surrounding Egypt were affected too. Back in the land of Canaan, Joseph's family was about to starve. When Jacob heard there was grain in Egypt, he sent his sons on a journey to buy food there.

As the story unfolds, the brothers who had once tried to kill Joseph end up standing before him seeking food to save their lives and the lives of their families. But they didn't recognize Joseph, now a grown man, and no doubt splendidly clothed in garments befitting a high-ranking Egyptian official. Joseph, however, recognized them. As the second most powerful man in Egypt, Joseph was in a position to pay his brothers back for what they did to him.

Author Marty Solomon, host of *The BEMA Podcast*, took a poignant look at this pivotal moment in Joseph's life. He said that as Joseph stands before his brothers he must decide who he really is:

Is Joseph a member of this family of God?...
Or is Joseph a part of Pharaoh's family?... Is he
going to be a person of vengeance? Because he
has his family right where he wants them. If
he wants to take it out on them he's got every
opportunity now.... Or is he going to be a person
of forgiveness? The Hebrew word here (for
forgiveness) they speak of is *hesed*—(a word
that also means) love, compassion, generosity,
forgiveness. Who is Joseph going to be?[29]

Joseph remembered the dreams he had when he was
a teenager, and seemed to waver a bit, as if deciding
what to do. He asked the brothers questions about
their family. They told him that they are all sons of
one man in the land of Canaan, that their youngest
brother is at home with their father, and that another
brother "is no more." Joseph then set up a condition
that the brothers must meet if they want enough grain
to save their families: one brother must stay behind in
Egypt while the others go home and bring back their
youngest brother. Joseph ensured that they had enough
grain for the journey home, and they eventually return
to Egypt with Benjamin, the youngest brother.

There is much more to this ancient story, but in the
end, with weeping and great emotion, Joseph reveals
his identity to his brothers and forgives them. Then

all sixty-six members of Joseph's extended family—his father Jacob, his brothers and sisters and their families—relocated to Egypt, bringing their livestock and all their household goods. Joseph used his authority to settle them in the best part of the land and provided food to sustain them all.

Reflecting on the end of this story, Marty Solomon focused on Joseph's decision to forgive. He said, "For you to lay down your right to vengeance and lay down your right to get even ... is one of the most ultimate acts of trust because you're saying 'God's got this. I can trust that God's got this.' Forgiveness is the ultimate expression of trust in this story."

> "To lay down your right to vengeance ... is one of the most ultimate acts of trust because you're saying 'God's got this.'"
> MARTY SOLOMON

Joseph was able to forgive his brothers because he finally understood that their wrongs against him were actually part of God's plan. He was meant to be God's point person in saving the world—and his own family—from famine. He could now look back and see that the wrongs he suffered put him in the right place at the right time to accomplish that. When he forgave his brothers, he told them, "You intended to harm me, but God intended it all for good. He brought me to this position so I could save the lives of many people."[30]

God's plan for your life stretches from the moment you were conceived to the day you will take your last breath. As you grapple with the wrongs done to you along the way, remember that in some mysterious way, God causes everything we experience to work together for our good and according to his purpose for our lives.[31] Hang onto the truth that forgiveness is the ultimate expression of your trust that he is doing this for you, just as he did for Joseph.

Resources

Books about how to forgive
The Art of Forgiving: When You Need to Forgive and Don't Know How by Lewis B. Smedes (Ballantine Books, 1996)

The Five Apology Languages: The Secret to Healthy Relationships by Gary Chapman and Jennifer Thomas (Northfield Publishing, 2022)

True story of forgiveness
The Hiding Place by Corrie ten Boom and Elizabeth Sherrill (Chosen Books, 2006)

Fictional story of forgiveness
The Shack by William P. Young (Windblown Media: 2008)

Website on relationships and well-being
Dr. Henry Cloud www.drcloud.com

Acknowledgments

Every book is a team effort in some way and this little book is no exception. Thanks go first of all to David, Marci, and Kara for sharing their personal forgiveness stories with me. Their names and some of the details of their experiences have been changed to protect the privacy of their families. I changed some minor aspects of my own stories for the same reason. I also want to thank Bible teacher Jerry Morrison and pastor Dr. Gary Chapman for reviewing the manuscript for biblical accuracy and for sharing excellent suggestions.

Notes

1   William Paul Young, *The Shack* (Windblown Media, 2007).

2   Lewis B. Smedes, "Forgiveness: The Power to Change the Past," *Christianity Today* (January 7, 1983), 22–26.

3   T. D. Jakes, "Lessons on Forgiveness from T. D. Jakes," *Tell Me More*, NPR Radio (April 5, 2012).

4   Tony Evans, "The Detours to Pardon," July 15, 2023, *Sermons Online*. https://sermons-online.org/tony -evans/the-detours-to-pardon.

5   Jakes, "Lessons on Forgiveness."

6   Henry Cloud and John Townsend, "How to Forgive When It's Hard to Forget," March 3, 2022, www.boundariesbooks.com/blogs/boundaries-blog /how-to-forgive-when-its-hard-to-forget.

7   Kirsten Weir, "Forgiveness Can Improve Mental and Physical Health," *American Psychological Association,* vol. 48 no. 1 (January 2017).

8   Loren L. Toussaint, Grant S. Shields, and George M. Slavich, "Forgiveness, Stress, and Health: a 5-Week Dynamic Parallel Process Study," *Annals of Behavioral Medicine* 50(5) (October 2016): 727–735.

9   "Forgiveness: Your Health Depends on It," *Johns Hopkins Medicine*. www.hopkinsmedicine.org/health /wellness-and-prevention/forgiveness-your-health -depends-on-it.

10 "Forgiveness: Letting Go of Grudges and Bitterness," *Mayo Clinic,* November 22, 2022. www.mayoclinic .org/healthy-lifestyle/adult-health/in-depth/forgiveness /art-20047692.

11 John Piper, "The Gospel in 6 Minutes," *Desiring God.* September 12, 2007. www.desiringgod.org/articles/the -gospel-in-6-minutes.

12 Smedes, "Forgiveness: The Power to Change the Past."

13 Amy Morin, "A Sample of Family Household Rules," *Verywell Family.* Updated October 5, 2022. www.verywellfamily.com/examples-of-household -rules-for-the-entire-family-1094879

14 Weir, "Forgiveness Can Improve Mental and Physical Health."

15 Smedes, "Forgiveness: The Power to Change the Past."

16 Jessica Cussins, "Involuntary Sterilization Then and Now," *Psychology Today.* September 5, 2013. www.psychologytoday.com/us/blog/genetic-crossroads /201309/involuntary-sterilization-then-and-now.

17 "The Power of Forgiveness," *Harvard Health Publishing.* February 12, 2021. www.health.harvard .edu/mind-and-mood/the-power-of-forgiveness.

18 Weir, "Forgiveness Can Improve Mental and Physical Health."

19 These studies cited in Rebecca A. Clay, "Don't Cry Over Spilled Milk—The Research on Why it's Important to Give Yourself a Break," *Monitor on Psychology* (September 2016): 70–72.

20 Ryan Howes, "Forgiveness vs. Reconciliation," *Psychology Today*. March 31, 2013. www.psychologytoday.com/us/blog/in-therapy /201303/forgiveness-vs-reconciliation.

21 Smedes, "Forgiveness: The Power to Change the Past."

22 Kayt Sukel, "Beyond Emotion: Understanding the Amygdala's Role in Memory," *The Dana Foundation*. March 13, 2018. www.dana.org/article/beyond -emotion-understanding-the-amygdalas-role-in-memory.

23 "The Vibrancy of Memories Fades With Time," *Association for Psychological Science*. April 29, 2019. www.psychologicalscience.org/publications/observer /obsonline/memory-vibrancy-fades.html.

24 Lewis B. Smedes, *The Art of Forgiving* (Ballentine Books, 1997).

25 "The Power of Forgiveness," *Harvard Health*.

26 Smedes quoted in Howes, "Forgiveness vs. Reconciliation."

27 Eugene E. Carpenter and Wayne McCown, gen. eds., *Asbury Bible Commentary* (Zondervan, 1992).

28 Worth Kilcrease, "Time Heals All Wounds, or Does it?" *Psychology Today*. April 24, 2008. www.psychologytoday.com/us/blog/the-journey -ahead/200804/time-heals-all-wounds-or-does-it.

29 Marty Solomon, "Out of the Pit," *BEMA Discipleship Podcast*, January 26, 2017. www.bemadiscipleship .com/16.

30 Genesis 50:20 NLT.

31 Romans 8:28.

About the Author

 Debbie Barr is an author, health educator, and speaker with a passion for encouraging people to engage deeply with God as they journey through tough times.

She earned her bachelor's degree in journalism from the Pennsylvania State University and her master's degree in health education from East Carolina University. A master certified health education specialist (MCHES®), Debbie is especially interested in health and wellness, health literacy, and Christian growth.

She lives in Bermuda Run, North Carolina.

You can learn more about Debbie by visiting her website (debbiebarr.com), her Amazon author page (amazon.com/author/debbiebarr) or her Linkedin profile (www.linkedin.com/in/debbiebarr).

Hope and Healing

www.hendricksonrose.com